PRESENT

A CHRISTMAS PAGEANT
Coloring Book

ILLUSTRATED BY JODIE McCALLUM

The Standard Publishing Company, Cincinnati, Ohio
A division of Standex International Corporation
© 1997 by The Standard Publishing Company. Printed in the United States of America
All rights reserved. ISBN 0-7847-0705-7
Designed by Coleen Davis

Jesus was born in a stable.

Mary was His mother. She took good care of baby Jesus.

Baby Jesus slept in a manger filled with hay.

Joseph helped care for the baby.

There were animals in the stable, donkeys and cows and sheep.

An angel told shepherds that Jesus was born!

The shepherds hurried to see the baby.

They found Him lying in a manger, just as the angel had told them.

Far away, wise men saw a new star in the sky.

They followed the star toward Bethlehem. It was a long journey.

At last the star stopped over the house where Jesus was.

The wise men worshiped little Jesus and gave Him gifts.